W9-CEW-389

# THE COLUMBINE
# SHOOTINGS

Essential Events

# THE COLUMBINE
# SHOOTINGS

BY DIANE MARCZELY GIMPEL

**Content Consultant**
Dr. Glenn Muschert, PhD, Associate Professor of Sociology,
Miami University

**ABDO**
Publishing Company

# CREDITS

Published by ABDO Publishing Company, PO Box 398166,
Minneapolis, MN 55439. Copyright © 2012 by Abdo Consulting
Group, Inc. International copyrights reserved in all countries. No
part of this book may be reproduced in any form without written
permission from the publisher. The Essential Library™ is a
trademark and logo of ABDO Publishing Company.

Printed in the United States of America,
North Mankato, Minnesota
092011
012012

 THIS BOOK CONTAINS AT LEAST 10% RECYCLED MATERIALS.

Editors: Lisa Owings
Copy Editor: Mari Kesselring
Cover design: Marie Tupy
Interior design and production: Kazuko Collins

**Library of Congress Cataloging-in-Publication Data**
Gimpel, Diane Marczely.
  The Columbine shootings / by Diane Marczely Gimpel.
    p. cm. -- (Essential events)
  Includes bibliographical references.
  ISBN 978-1-61783-308-3
  1. Columbine High School Massacre, Littleton, Colo.,
1999--Juvenile literature.  I. Title.
  LB3013.33.C6G56 2012
  373.17'820978882--dc23

                              2011038453

# TABLE OF CONTENTS

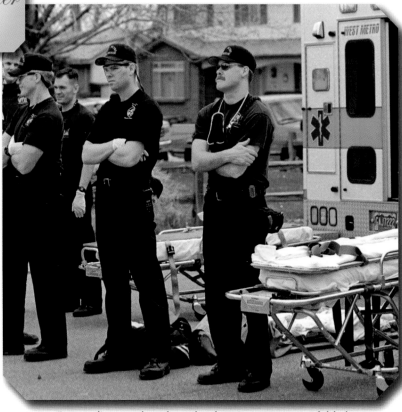

*Paramedics stood ready as the shooting rampage unfolded inside the school.*

# Tragedy Strikes
## a US High School

On April 20, 1999, emergency physician Dr. Christopher Colwell was at Columbine High School in suburban Jefferson County, Colorado. He spent most of the afternoon helping students and teachers who had been injured in a brutal attack earlier that day. Two senior students had fired guns and detonated explosives at the school. But by 4:30 p.m. the terrible assault was over, and another job had to be done.

Escorted by SWAT team members, Colwell walked into the school building. He looked for signs of life in the library, where the killers had done their deadliest shooting. He did not find any. Instead, Colwell saw lifeless body after lifeless body. One body was slumped by a computer, but most were on the floor, one clutching a pencil. Colwell found the bodies of 12 students inside the school. Ten of them were victims. Two of them were the gunmen, who had turned their guns on themselves after killing the others. From the library, Colwell went to a science classroom, where he found the body of a teacher who bled to death after one of the gunmen shot him. "It's the most difficult scene I've ever encountered," Colwell said later. "Horror would be the best way to describe it. They never addressed this in medical school."[1]

Colwell's purpose on the site then changed from offering aid to establishing the official time of death. At approximately 4:45 p.m. Colwell pronounced the two gunmen, the gunmen's ten victims in the library, and the teacher dead. Already Colwell had pronounced two students who had been shot outside the school building dead. More than 20 other victims had been wounded.

This deadly shooting is now referred to as "Columbine," after the high school where it occurred. At the time, it had the most fatalities of any school shooting in US history. The event provoked widespread fear as students wondered whether the same thing could happen at their schools. Parents wondered if their children were in danger at school. That fear prompted efforts for change. School

## Other School Shootings

The Columbine tragedy remains the worst US high school shooting, but is not the worst US school massacre. That infamy belongs to the May 18, 1927, disaster at Bath Consolidated School, a grades-two-through-six school in Bath Township, Michigan. Andrew Kehoe, a 46-year-old farmer and school board member, used explosives to kill 45 people, including himself, that day. Of those 45, 38 were elementary schoolchildren. Fifty-eight people were hurt.

Another school shooting listed with Columbine among the nation's deadliest happened on August 1, 1966. That day Charles Whitman shot people from the 28-story tower at the University of Texas at Austin. Whitman killed 16 people and wounded 31 others before Austin police killed him.

The deadliest US school shooting happened April 16, 2007, on the campus of Virginia Polytechnic Institute and State University in Blacksburg, Virginia. There, Cho Seung-Hui, a 23-year-old senior English major, killed 32 people and himself. The Virginia Tech killings came four days before the eight-year anniversary of the Columbine shootings.

security measures increased and tightened nationwide. Schools created antiviolence programs and antibullying programs in reaction to reports that the gunmen had sought revenge against bullies.

Law enforcement officials also made some changes. Police modified the way they would respond to similar attacks. Stopping the shooter became the highest priority. Law enforcement authorities studied the characteristics of school shooters to create a shooter profile. They hoped this would help prevent similar atrocities in the future. Gun control advocates proposed changes to toughen gun laws.

## STUDENTS REACT

The first to react to the shootings were the students, teachers, and others on the Columbine campus that sunny spring day. The attack began at 11:19 a.m., when black-garbed students Eric Harris and Dylan Klebold pulled guns from duffel bags and began firing. They started shooting at students eating outside, then continued their rampage inside the school. Students and teachers who were able to escape the school did so, while others tried hiding inside. Some hid in cupboards. Some hid in the ceiling.

*Ten of the 12 students killed in the shooting were killed in the library.*

News reporters learned of the shootings around 11:30 a.m. by listening to police scanners. They soon arrived at the scene, where they talked to those who were able to get out of the building. "We hid in the counseling office," Columbine senior Annie Ford said. "I was peeking out the window and saw everybody sprinting, crying, crawling on the floor."[2] An unnamed student said:

*We saw three people get shot. They were just shooting. They didn't care who they shot. They were just shooting. We didn't think it was real and then we saw blood.*[3]

Rachel Erbert, a 17-year-old senior, told a reporter:

*I saw [a teacher] on the floor bleeding from everywhere. He was trying to direct kids, but he couldn't talk. It was really scary. Kids were falling, and you'd help them up. I thought I might get shot.*[4]

The library was the scene of the most carnage. Amanda Stair, a 15-year-old sophomore, hid with other students under the tables there. "Two guys in black trench coats walked in," she recounted. "They said get up or they would shoot us. I heard a lot of shots and one guy put his gun down on the desk I was under."[5] The library smelled of gunpowder, and students were crying and screaming there, Stair said. Bree Pasquale, a junior who was not shot but was splattered with the blood of another student, told a news reporter the gunmen were so mentally disturbed that they seemed to be having fun during their terror spree. "You could hear them laughing as they ran down the hallways, shooting people."[6]

## THE NATION WATCHES

By noon, the local television stations in the Denver area were showing uninterrupted coverage of the tragedy. A local television helicopter began beaming live shots from outside the school at approximately 12:05 p.m. Soon live shots of what was happening at Columbine were broadcast nationwide. Millions of people watched as the tragedy unfolded. Television coverage showed students and teachers running from the school and SWAT teams organizing. Television cameras also captured injured student Patrick Ireland flopping out of a second-floor library window into the arms of SWAT members who were standing on the roof of an armored vehicle.

US President Bill Clinton was among those to whom reports of Columbine reached. During a previously scheduled news conference that afternoon on an unrelated matter, the president asked Americans to pray for the students,

**Tears of Relief**

Some tears shed following the shooting came from parents relieved to find their children among the living. Kristie Vest wept when she was reunited with her daughter and niece. Another woman sobbed when she reached a loved one by cell phone. "Oh, God! You're safe!" she screamed.[7]

*Friends and family of Columbine students gathered outside the school, hoping to reunite with and comfort their loved ones.*

parents, and teachers of Columbine. Clinton later noted that if such a thing could happen in suburban Colorado, it could happen anywhere in the country.

## WHY?

In addition to sympathizing with the Columbine community, people across the country also wondered what had caused the boys to unleash such terror. Survivors heard the gunmen offer different reasons for what they were doing. Some said the boys emulated Nazis. As it turned out, the killing spree happened on what would have been Adolf Hitler's 110th birthday. Student Bree Pasquale said one of the gunmen told her the massacre was revenge for being made fun of in the past. This comment led some to blame the killers' actions on bullying. Another student reported the gunmen shot a girl because she was praying to God. Still another said the gunmen shot a boy because he was black. Some students also reported the gunmen said they were after "jocks." Another student told reporters the boys simply hated the whole school. Some attributed the boys' violence to their love of violent movies and video games. Still others said the boys shot at people randomly. It would take thorough investigation into Klebold's and Harris's lives leading up to that day to get some answers. ⌐

**The Prequels**

The Columbine shootings came during a two-year period when a rash of such episodes seemed to occur. Three fatal school shootings happened in 1997 and four in 1998. They included a shooting on December 1, 1997, when 14-year-old Michael Corneal killed three classmates and wounded five others at a West Paducah, Kentucky, high school.

*The killers videotaped themselves at a makeshift shooting range several weeks before the attack.*

*A video Harris, left, and Klebold made for a school project shows them dressed in black trench coats, pretending to shoot and kill school bullies.*

# THE BOYS AND THE BOMBING

Columbine killers Eric David Harris and Dylan Bennet Klebold had childhoods similar to many other middle-class American boys, but their lives took deadly turns in their late teen years. Both Harris, born April 9, 1981, and Klebold, born September 11, 1981, played soccer and baseball when they were little. In elementary school, Klebold was in a program for gifted students. Harris moved around a bit with his family because his father was in the military at the time. As the boys got older, both Harris and Klebold developed an interest in computers. Klebold even built his own home computer. The boys met in middle school.

When they started at Columbine High School, the boys carried their interest in computers with them. Harris enjoyed the school's computer labs. Klebold was a school computer assistant, helping to maintain Columbine's computer network. He planned to be a computer science major in college. Harris and Klebold were also involved in school video productions and Columbine's Rebel News Network. Outside school, both boys worked at the same pizza restaurant. Harris, who was known as Reb (short for Rebel), had other friends in high school. However, Klebold, who was known as VoDKa (he capitalized his initials in the word) was shy and was described as a follower with few close friends other than Harris.

Both boys tended to dress in black and were thought by some to be members of the Trench Coat

Mafia. This loosely knit group of young people was known for wearing long, black coats to school and for playing video games, including the shooting game *Doom*, for which Harris programmed some of his own additional levels. Reports conflict over whether the boys were part of the group, however. Some said members of the group had already graduated from Columbine. Some students told investigators that those associated with the Trench Coat Mafia were teased by other students—by athletes in particular. But while some said students picked on the boys, Columbine senior Noelle Porter disputed that. "Everyone's saying that people were always after them," Porter said. "But it wasn't that way at all. It was the opposite. They didn't really seem to like other people."[1]

## Trouble with the Law

In most respects, Harris and Klebold appeared to be living fairly unremarkable teen lives prior to the Columbine attack, though they once ran afoul

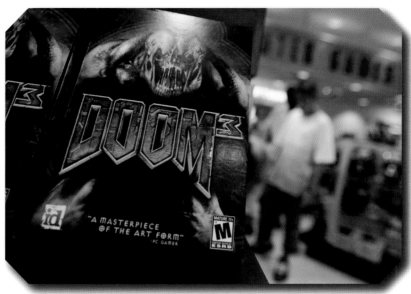

*The killers loved the violent video game Doom,*
*in which the player has the perspective of a shooter.*

of the law. On January 30, 1998, they were arrested
for breaking into a van and stealing electronics.
They were placed in a special program for juveniles
who break the law. In this program, their records
would be wiped clean after they completed certain
requirements, such as paying fines, attending anger
management classes, undergoing counseling, and
doing community service. Harris and Klebold
were successful in the juvenile diversion program.
The charges against them were dropped on
February 9, 1999.

Harris had a near miss with authorities in March 1998 when Randy Brown, father of Columbine student Brooks Brown, reported Harris to the Jefferson County Sheriff's Office. Randy Brown said Harris made death threats against Brooks on his Web site. Harris also allegedly wrote on his Web site about making and blowing up bombs and targeting people with them. But authorities could not access the Web site or verify the bomb detonation claims. The Browns also feared retribution and wanted to remain anonymous. So, the investigation ended. Harris later reconciled with Brooks and warned him to get away from the school just before Harris began his attack on Columbine.

## The Dark Plan

A year before the shooting, Harris and Klebold made entries in each other's 1998 yearbooks that suggested they were already planning their attack. In Harris's yearbook, Klebold wrote about "the holy April morning of NBK."[3] NBK is an acronym for *Natural Born Killers,* a movie about lovers who are serial killers. Klebold also wrote about "killing enemies, blowing up stuff, killing cops" and that they would take revenge in the commons, another name for

JC-001-026029

*Harris and Klebold left behind nearly 1,000 pages of drawings and writings that illustrate their obsession with violence and preparation for the shooting.*

Columbine's cafeteria.[4] Investigators speculated the revenge Klebold sought was for the pair's January 1998 arrest. Harris also referenced NBK in his yearbook message to Klebold. He drew a gunman amid dead bodies and wrote: "God I can't wait till they die. I can taste the blood now."[5]

Their plan was to blow up the Columbine High School cafeteria with timer-detonated, propane-fueled bombs during the busy first lunch period, killing as many people as possible. As the bombs exploded, Klebold and Harris would be armed and waiting outside to shoot any survivors trying to get away. Finally, bombs in the boys' cars, parked in the school parking lot near the cafeteria, would explode to kill whoever responded to the crisis.

## MAKING THE PLAN A REALITY

The teens used their earnings from their part-time pizza shop jobs to put their plans into action. The limited income probably limited the carnage, contended David Cullen, who wrote a book called *Columbine* about the tragedy. A bigger factor in keeping the death toll down would be the poor wiring on the propane bombs, which did not explode.

Approximately six months before the attack, Harris began building pipe bombs and other explosive devices. Eventually he and Klebold made approximately 100 bombs. They also wanted guns. As minors, they would need the help of others to get them. Robyn Anderson was 18 years old and Klebold's date for the prom held three nights before the

### Explosive Devices

One inventory record Harris made of the explosives he had for the attack included 53 "crickets," which were small explosives like grenades, and 24 pipe bombs. But there were more. Authorities later counted 30 exploded devices at Columbine, two diversionary devices off campus, and 67 unexploded devices at the school, in the killers' cars, and at the killers' homes.

attack. She bought the boys a rifle and two shotguns at a gun show in November 1998. In January 1999, Klebold bought a TEC-DC9 semiautomatic pistol for $500 from Mark Manes, a 22-year-old man Harris and Klebold met at a gun show. Phil Duran, a 22-year-old who also worked at the pizza shop, introduced them. Both Manes and Duran were later charged with providing a handgun to minors.

In April 1999, Harris and Klebold videotaped their weapons and bombs in Harris's bedroom. They conducted dress rehearsals of their plan, which they also videotaped.

### April 20

It is unclear what significance, if any, can be assigned to the date Harris and Klebold chose for the attack. Some indications are that the boys planned the attack for April 19 but put it off for a day because they hadn't finished their preparations. April 19, 1999, would have been the sixth anniversary of a deadly confrontation between the federal government and the Branch Davidian religious cult near Waco, Texas. April 19, 1999, also was the fourth anniversary of the bombing of a federal office building in Oklahoma perpetrated by US terrorists in reaction to the Waco episode. It is not known if either event was relevant to the boys.

April 20, the day of the attack, was the 110th anniversary of the birth of Adolf Hitler, the genocidal dictator of Germany who instigated World War II (1939–1945). Harris drew swastikas—a symbol adopted by Hitler's Nazi political party—in his journal. Some students said the boys wore swastikas and were aware of Hitler's birthday. Nonetheless, authorities are not sure that was behind the date's selection. April 20 is also a date associated with marijuana use.

They even taped themselves driving to the store to buy supplies for the attack.

On April 19, the day before the attack, Klebold wrote in his math notebook:

> About 26.5 hours from now the judgment will begin. Difficult but not impossible, necessary, nerve-racking, and fun. What fun is life without a little death? It's interesting, when I'm in my human form, knowing I'm going to die. Everything has a touch of triviality to it.[6]

Klebold also created a schedule for the next day's bombing. So did Harris. Klebold's schedule indicated the pair planned to set up bombs in the school at 11:09 a.m. to go off at 11:17 a.m. They planned to set the bombs in their cars to go off at 11:18 a.m. Then they would wait outside the school. Klebold wrote: "When first bombs go off, attack. have fun!"[7] Harris's schedule called for setting up duffel bags containing bombs at 11:10 a.m. and then going outside to wait near their cars. Next to the notation for 11:16 a.m., the minute before the first bombs were set to explode, Harris wrote, "HAHAHA."[8]

*Harris and Klebold worked as cooks at a pizza place. The owner, pictured here, said they seemed like normal high school kids.*

*Brooks Brown, a childhood friend of Klebold, was spared by Harris, who had once threatened him.*

# APRIL 20, 1999

"Go! Go!"[1]

That is the shout students heard outside Columbine High School at approximately 11:19 a.m. on April 20, 1999, as Harris and Klebold began their violent rampage. In the next 15 minutes or so, Harris and Klebold killed 12 students and one teacher and physically injured more than 20 other people, some of them seriously and permanently. Not long after that, the gunmen turned their guns on themselves.

TROUBLE ARRIVES

The tragedy began at approximately 11:10 a.m. on that sunny Tuesday, according to a chronology compiled by the Jefferson County Sheriff's Office. Harris arrived at school in his gray 1986 Honda Civic, followed shortly by Klebold, who arrived in a black 1982 BMW. The boys parked their cars on either side of the school's cafeteria, near doors to the school's lower level. Outside one of the entrances, Harris saw Brooks Brown, the boy he had once threatened to kill. Harris gave him a warning: "Brooks, I like you now. Get out of here. Go home."[2] Brown left.

At approximately 11:14 a.m., Harris and Klebold entered the school cafeteria dressed in long, black coats. There they left duffel bags containing 20-pound (9-kg) propane bombs set to explode at 11:17 a.m., which was during the school's first lunch shift. The cafeteria would be filled with students.

After dropping the duffel bags, Harris and Klebold returned to their cars to await detonation. But the bombs did not explode. So Harris and Klebold went back toward the school building. It was then that one of them yelled, "Go! Go!"[3]

## THE SHOOTING BEGINS

Both boys pulled sawed-off shotguns out of another set of duffel bags and began shooting. Rachel Scott and Richard Castaldo were eating lunch outside on the grass. They became Harris and Klebold's first victims. Rachel was killed. Richard was seriously wounded. Harris and Klebold then shot at other students who were outside. Those hit included Daniel Rohrbough, Sean Graves, Lance Kirklin, Michael Johnson, and Mark Taylor. Harris killed Daniel, shooting him five times. Freshman Adam Thomas heard bullets whiz past his ears. Harris shot Anne Marie

### The Weapons

On April 20, 1999, Klebold carried a 9 mm semiautomatic handgun and a 12-gauge double-barreled shotgun. Harris carried a 9 mm carbine rifle and a 12-gauge pump shotgun. Both boys used both of their guns, firing 188 shots altogether. They also equipped themselves with shotgun shells, 9 mm bullet clips, knives, and bombs. Tragically, the boys were able to acquire these weapons without arousing suspicion. Many believe stricter gun control laws would have prevented the shooting.

Hochhalter several times as she tried to run inside the school to hide in the cafeteria.

The noise and chaos attracted the attention of students in the cafeteria. Some students moved toward the cafeteria windows to find out what was happening outside. The commotion also got the attention of adults at the school, including teacher William "Dave" Sanders and a couple of custodians, who began trying to get the students to safety. "Get down! Get under a table," yelled a custodian.[4] Then someone else yelled "crawl" and the students did that until they got out of the cafeteria.[5] Then they ran.

Teacher Patricia Nielson was patrolling the school halls. She made her way to the west entrance to tell the boys she thought were holding toy guns to stop. A shower of glass and metal fragments hit her when one of the boys fired into that entrance. Also hit was student Brian Anderson, who was trying to get out of the school on the advice of another teacher. Both Nielson and Brian ran upstairs to hide in the school library. Nielson called 911 for help just as Sheriff's Deputy Neil Gardner arrived to respond to a previous 911 call from the school. Harris and Gardner shot at each other. Then Harris went into the school. Moments later, Deputy Paul Smoker

A security camera captured this image of Harris and Klebold, who was carrying a TEC-DC9 semiautomatic pistol through the school cafeteria.

arrived to help Gardner. Harris leaned out a broken window to exchange gunfire with Smoker before again retreating into the school.

Students began leaving the school—apparently at teacher Sanders's urging—through an exit on the opposite side of the building from Klebold and Harris. The boys began firing their weapons in school hallways, hitting lockers and other objects as students ran away. One student, Stephanie Munson, was shot in the ankle as she ran out of the school.

The gunmen headed for the library hallway, where they encountered Sanders at approximately 11:26 a.m. They shot him, wounding him fatally, though Sanders would live for a few more hours. Sanders managed to crawl to another hallway, where a teacher pulled him into a classroom.

## THE LIBRARY

Klebold and Harris spent a few minutes firing randomly in the library hallway and lighting and tossing small bombs. Then, at 11:29 a.m., they walked into the library and yelled, "Get up!"[6] Fifty-two students, many of them hiding under library tables, and four staff members were there. No one obeyed the order. One of the gunmen said, "Fine. I'll start shooting."[7] Both boys did. Harris fired shots along a counter, causing splinters to injure student Evan Todd. Klebold killed Kyle Velasquez, who was sitting at a computer table. Klebold and Harris fired out the library windows at law enforcement officers and at students. Inside the library, Klebold shot Daniel Steepleton, Makai Hall, and Patrick Ireland. Patrick was shot a second time when he tried to help other students. Harris killed Steven Curnow and wounded Kacey Reugsegger, both of whom were hiding under a computer table. Harris moved on to another table and killed Cassie Bernall, one of the two girls hiding beneath it. Then he terrorized Bree Pasquale, asking her if she wanted to die. She pleaded for her life. "Everyone's gonna die," Harris said. "We're gonna blow up the school anyway."[8]

Firing under another table, Harris killed Isaiah Shoels. Klebold killed Matthew Kechter. With his subsequent shots, Klebold wounded Mark Kintgen, Valeen Schnurr, and Lisa Kreutz. He killed Lauren Townsend. Valeen, weeping, called out: "Oh God,

## Who Said Yes?

Within days of the Columbine shootings, news outlets reported one of the killers asked Cassie Bernall if she believed in God and then shot her to death after she said yes. The story came from other students who were in the library with her during the rampage. The martyrdom story traveled widely by way of media reports and the book *She Said Yes: The Unlikely Martyrdom of Cassie Bernall,* a memoir of Cassie written by her mother. The story caused a surge in the recruitment of young people by Christian organizations.

Just after the book came out, however, news outlets reported the exchange probably did not happen, a finding later supported by the Jefferson County Sheriff's Office. The office's report on the shootings indicated Harris bent down to look under the table where Cassie was hiding with another student, slapped the top of the table twice, said "Peek-a-boo," and shot Cassie to death.[9] The report said Klebold taunted another student, Valeen Schnurr, about her belief in God after he critically wounded her, and then he walked away. Emily Wyant, the student who was under the library table with Cassie, said Cassie prayed but did not exchange words with her killer.

help me!"[10] According to the sheriff's report, Klebold taunted her about her belief in God and then walked away. "I didn't see his face. . . . But their voices . . . it was like they were happy. To them it was like playing a game," Valeen said, describing the scene years later.[11]

Harris shot Nicole Nowlen and John Tomlin. When John came out from his hiding spot under a table, Klebold killed him. Harris next killed Kelly Fleming. Harris shot Lauren Townsend and Lisa Kreutz again. He shot Jeanna Park. Then Harris killed Daniel Mauser. Both teens then shot under another table, wounding Jennifer Doyle and Stephen Austin Eubanks and killing Corey DePooter.

## THE END FOR KLEBOLD AND HARRIS

In less than eight minutes, Harris and Klebold killed ten people

### Rohrbough, Tomlin, and Velasquez

Fifteen-year-old Daniel Rohrbough worked in his father's business after school and worked during the summer on his grand-father's farm in Kansas. He used the money he earned to buy Christmas presents for his family members. Victim John Tomlin was a 16-year-old sophomore with plans to join the US Army after high school. A year before his murder, John had gone on a mission trip to Mexico, where he helped build a house for a needy family. Sixteen-year-old Kyle Velasquez experienced cognitive challenges because of a stroke he suffered during infancy. His uncle said, "Kyle was known as a gentle giant."[12]

## Curnow, DePooter, and Kechter

Fourteen-year-old Columbine freshman Steven Curnow was a soccer player and referee as well as a fan of *Star Wars* movies. Seventeen-year-old Corey DePooter was an athlete who planned to join the US Marine Corps after graduation. Matthew Kechter, a 16-year-old sophomore, was a junior varsity lineman and an A student. He had planned to study engineering and attend the University of Colorado after graduation.

and wounded 12 others. They left the library, made their way to the science area, and then went back to the cafeteria, throwing pipe bombs and shooting their guns along the way. They partially detonated one of the bombs in the cafeteria but did not injure anyone else physically. "Today the world's going to come to an end," one of the gunmen said. "Today we're going to die."[13] Then they returned to the library where, after shooting through the windows at law enforcement officers, they killed themselves. It was 12:08 p.m. The gunmen were dead, but the ordeal was not over.

*Evacuated students searched for their friends and comforted one another.*

*A SWAT team moves toward Columbine High School to perform a search of the school after the shooting rampage.*

# Law Enforcement Responds

Within three minutes of Klebold and Harris's first shots, Jefferson County Sheriff's Deputy Neil Gardner got a 911 call from a school custodian about trouble in the back parking lot. Gardner, who worked at the school, arrived at the scene within two minutes, but Harris and Klebold had already killed two students and had wounded several others outside the cafeteria. Two more deputies arrived in response to Gardner's call for help and began attending to wounded students outside the school. As the sounds of gunfire reverberated inside Columbine, people fled the school in panic. They told sheriff's deputies that gunmen wearing long, black coats were randomly shooting people and throwing explosives. Emergency radio dispatchers heard the same thing from people inside the school who called 911. Dispatchers could hear the sounds of gunfire and explosions on those calls. They broadcast an alert about a gunman in the school.

## SWAT Arrives

Just after 11:30 a.m., officers from surrounding communities arrived and SWAT teams were on their way. Law enforcement officers surrounded the building and covered all 25 exits within 15 minutes. Officers followed the protocol in place at the time: contain the threat and then wait for specially trained and equipped SWAT teams to neutralize the threat. SWAT teams arrived a few minutes later and at 11:52 a.m. got the order to enter the school immediately.

Law enforcement did not know Harris and Klebold had killed their last victim more than a half hour earlier and that the gunmen had committed suicide moments after the first SWAT team went into the school to find them. The scene was so chaotic it was hard to tell what was happening, and the attack seemed to go on for much longer than it actually did. One reason was that when SWAT members exploded locks to get inside locked classrooms for searches, students in hiding called for help on their cell phones, reporting explosions.

Additionally, the information law enforcers had was sketchy. Up to eight gunmen were reported in the building in locations that included the cafeteria, the library, the science rooms, the business office, the band room, and the catwalk in the auditorium. Some reports indicated the gunmen were holding hostages. Someone reported a sniper on the roof, although he was really just repairing the air conditioning. Furthermore, the SWAT teams did not know their way around the school. The SWAT commander's understanding of the school's layout was based on an old floor plan that showed the

*Columbine's cafeteria was the first area in the school subjected to the chaos and destruction of the shootings.*

cafeteria and library—the primary locations of the attack—on the other side of the school. However, the cafeteria and library had been moved during a relatively recent renovation.

Once inside, SWAT teams used hand signals to communicate because fire alarms triggered by the bombs blared so loudly. They had to break into locked classrooms to look for people. When they found them, they had to search them because they worried the shooters might try to blend in and escape along with the other students. They found some students shivering in kitchen freezers.

Others were standing in kitchen storage areas in ankle-deep water from fire sprinkler systems. In some cases, terrified students had to be talked into following the black-clad officers they thought could be the shooters.

It took about three hours for SWAT team members to reach the library. They entered at 3:22 p.m. They found the bodies of ten victims and the shooters as well as one wounded survivor, Lisa Kreutz, who paramedics evacuated and then sent to the hospital.

## A Wounded Teacher Awaits Help

Another person who initially survived his gunshot wounds, teacher William "Dave" Sanders, did not make it until paramedics arrived. Sanders had been pulled into a second-floor science classroom after being shot shortly before 11:30 a.m. Eagle Scouts Aaron Hancey and Kevin Starkey administered first aid to Sanders, supplementing what they knew with instructions Aaron got over the phone from paramedics. Others in the classroom called 911 for help, too. Law enforcement first learned of Sanders's situation at 11:45 a.m., approximately 15 minutes after Sanders was shot.

Jefferson County's timeline of the episode indicates that by 12:14 p.m., a dispatcher had been on the telephone for some time with students in the school who were with a wounded teacher. Dispatchers told the students and teachers help was "on the way" and asked them to tie a shirt on the classroom doorknob to help SWAT teams find them.[1] In addition, at about noon, a teacher wrote "I BLEEDING TO DEATH" on a whiteboard and put it in a window.[2]

At approximately 2:45 p.m., a SWAT team evacuated the 60 students in the science room and requested medical assistance for Sanders. It took another 20 minutes or so for a paramedic to get to Sanders, who, at that point, had died.

### Eagle Scouts Try to Save a Teacher

To help Sanders after he was shot, Aaron Hancey, a junior and an Eagle Scout, used his own T-shirt to slow the blood flow. He used other boys' shirts to make bandages, tourniquets, and a pillow. Aaron called his father, who called 911 and relayed the paramedics' instructions over the phone. Aaron got additional help from fellow Eagle Scout Kevin Starkey, who took turns pressing Sanders's wounds to stem the blood loss. They used blankets from the science classroom's first-aid closet to keep Sanders warm.

The boys also offered Sanders encouragement: "You're doing all right. They're coming. Just hold on. You can do it."[3] They pulled family photos from his wallet and showed them to him, asking questions as they went along: "Is this your wife?" "What's her name?" They talked to him about his family. "These people love you," they said. "This is why you need to live."[4]

*Aaron Hancey and Kevin Starkey used their Eagle Scout training to administer care to their teacher, Dave Sanders.*

## ZEROING IN ON THE KILLERS

Earlier in the afternoon, authorities seemed to have concluded who was behind the carnage. Sheriff's office documents show authorities had Harris's name before noon. It is unclear when they determined Klebold was working with him, but by 1:15 p.m., investigators arrived at each boy's home to search it. At Harris's house, investigators found live bombs and gasoline. They evacuated the neighbors before removing the explosives. Investigators found explosives at Klebold's house, too. They found Harris's and Klebold's explosive-laden cars in a Columbine parking lot around 4:00 p.m.

At approximately 4:45 p.m., when most of the victims had been pronounced dead, the initial SWAT search of the school was done. But authorities worked in the school throughout the night, looking for and neutralizing bombs and booby traps the shooters had placed throughout the school while on their rampage.

**The Search of Harris's House**

In addition to the bombs and gasoline found at Harris's home, investigators also found videotapes pertinent to the tragedy. In one, Harris and Klebold show their stockpile of explosives. In another, the boys discuss bomb construction. Investigators also found a notebook in which Harris inventoried the bombs he had built.

## OUTSIDE THE SCHOOL

As SWAT teams worked inside the school throughout the afternoon, much was going on outside, too. Bomb squads arrived. Paramedics helped the injured and sent them to area hospitals. News media reported on the tragedy. Parents descended upon the area and were directed to nearby Leawood Elementary School, where students were taken by bus after evacuation. Among the parents who did not have a reunion was Bruce Beck, Lauren Townsend's stepfather. "You see all the kids run out of the building," he said. "You're just sure one of the kids is going to be yours."[5]

That evening, authorities told parents ten bodies would be kept in the school overnight because bombs and booby traps were near them. Parents were asked to provide information to help the authorities identify their children, such as what clothes the students were wearing. At this, some left the room to be physically sick over the thought that their child could be dead. At approximately 8:00 p.m., Michael Shoels, father of Isaiah, said, "It's like a dream I'm trying to wake up from. Things are not looking good at all."[6] On April 21, the bodies were removed and identified and the parents were notified. Autopsies were done as part of the investigation. Although authorities knew who the shooters were at this point, the investigation continued into how and why they attacked.

**Isaiah Shoels**

Isaiah Shoels, an African-American student, had about a month to go before graduation when he was murdered. Witnesses of Isaiah's death say Harris uttered a racial slur before shooting him. Isaiah had told his parents that members of the Trench Coat Mafia had been harassing him because of his race. "My son had two strikes against him. He was black and he was an athlete. That's why my son died," said Isaiah's father.[7]

*A mother and daughter reuniting after the shooting*

*Candlelight vigils were held throughout the region.*

# SAYING GOOD-BYE

While authorities continued their investigations into the deadly shootings, families and friends of the deceased teacher and students as well as the public mourned the loss of life, the loss of normalcy, and the loss of a sense of security. The community mourned at a makeshift memorial near the school, memorial services in churches throughout the region, and community forums and candlelight vigils. There was also a large memorial service attended by Vice President Al Gore. Additionally, there were the funeral services for those who died.

Throughout the mourning, people kept asking the same question: Why did this happen? It was a question authorities wanted to answer too.

## CLEMENT PARK

The day after the tragedy, students began a makeshift memorial at Clement Park, adjacent to Columbine High School. By the weekend, hundreds of flowers and written messages were left to honor those who died. Students from the University of Denver brought 1,000 paper cranes they had made to the site. Some people left teddy bears and photographs. One boy brought a soccer ball in memory of Daniel Rohrbough. The two had played soccer together in seventh grade. "It's the way I remember him," said Colin Vorhees.[1] Some hung banners expressing their sentiments, including a simply worded one from Columbine alumni that said "Love, always, CHS alumni."[2] Other banners left room for people to leave their own messages. Among them were: "I grieve for the lost. Why and how?"[3]

At one point, 15 wooden crosses stood on a hill in the park—one for each murder victim and one for each dead murderer. Greg Zanis of Illinois built and installed the crosses, a Christian religious symbol. Soon after, Brian Rohrbough, father of one of the murder victims, took down the two crosses memorializing the shooters. This sparked debate

---

### Memorializing Harris and Klebold

When an Illinois man erected memorial crosses in a makeshift public shrine not only for those killed but also for the killers, controversy ensued. Some felt Harris and Klebold were victims of a society that failed them and they had acted out because of that. Others felt the killers did not deserve memorials, especially not in the same place as their victims.

Jean Carney of Denver put a note on Klebold's cross that said: "May God have mercy on your soul. Sorry we all failed you." He suggested the ills of society were to blame for what happened: "We allowed all this horrible violence on TV and the movies. The whole society failed them."[4] Sharon Dunn, a Littleton resident, said the crosses for Klebold and Harris showed "there isn't a hatred held against anybody."[5]

Another visitor to the memorials saw things differently, however. "I don't think it's right to have the killers up here with the victims," said Anna Whitcomb of Denver. "I don't think they should be recognized. I think it does an injustice. . . . People come here to mourn and to pay respect to the innocent victims. Dylan and Eric were not the innocent."[6]

over whether and how Harris and Klebold should be memorialized. Zanis drove back to the park a few days later and removed the rest of the crosses. "It's so much controversy," Zanis said.[7] He came back again, a few days later, to install just 13 crosses on the hill. But park officials did not issue a permit for the memorial, so Zanis took them down again. He moved them to an approved site nearby, where they became part of a temporary memorial.

## MEMORIAL SERVICES

In addition to visiting Clement Park, mourners showed their grief by wearing ribbons of blue and silver—Columbine High School's colors—and by attending myriad memorial services and candlelight vigils at places of worship throughout the region. The largest memorial service was held Sunday, April 25, 1999, in a movie theater parking lot not far from the high school. Seventy thousand people—more than double the number expected—attended the afternoon event. Among them were Vice President Al Gore, Colorado Governor Bill Owens, retired general Colin Powell, evangelist Franklin Graham, and musician Amy Grant.

*A controversial memorial site featured 15 crosses to represent all the deceased, including the shooters, whose crosses were covered in black.*

Gore spoke of the horror of the random killing of innocent people. He told the crowd:

> *Here in Jefferson County, the spring has yielded to a cold winter of the heart. I would be misleading you if I said I understand this. I don't. Why human beings do evil, I do not understand. Why bad things happen to good people, I do not understand.*[8]

Gore encouraged parents to rebel against a violent culture and the easy availability of guns and to help children cope with their problems in a safe and healthy way. "We need to look for the earliest signs of trouble—and teach our children to resolve their differences with reason and conscience, not with flashes of passion," Gore said.[9]

Governor Owens referenced evidence that Harris and Klebold had not been planning to shoot specific groups of people—such as athletes, blacks, bullies, and Christians—as originally thought. What they actually planned was to kill hundreds of people in an explosion. "As we learn more about this, we learn how short of their goal the killers fell," Owens said. "Yes, they took far too many precious lives. But they failed in their goal of killing hundreds more and to burn the school to the ground."[10]

As the service ended, four fighter jets flew over the crowd in a V shape with one jet pulling up and away in what is known as a Missing Man formation. Then 13 white doves were released—one for each of the slain victims—as Governor Owens read the victims' names. Klebold and Harris were not mentioned. Blue and silver balloons were also released into the sky.

## The Funerals

The funeral services for Harris and Klebold's victims were additional opportunities to grieve the lost. The first funeral service happened on Friday,

April 23, just three days after the shooting. Funerals continued through the middle of the following week and were attended by thousands of people. People across the country were able to see Rachel Scott's funeral because it was televised by CNN. Many wrote messages in black marker on Rachel's white casket, practically covering it with script. At Cassie Bernall's funeral, Cassie herself spoke by way of a church video she had made two days before she died. "I just try not to contradict myself, to get rid of all the hypocrisy and just live for Christ," she said.[11] The Roman Catholic archbishop of Denver presided over the double funeral of sophomores Kelly Ann Fleming and Daniel Mauser. "May they live radiant and forever young in the happiness of [God's] kingdom," Archbishop Charles J. Chaput said.[12] Lauren Townsend's brother spoke at his sister's funeral: "People say that Lauren was a victim. I don't think of her in that way. The ugly thing that happened last Tuesday, they couldn't conquer her beauty."[13]

At Dave Sanders's funeral, the teacher was remembered for helping

**Scott and Fleming**

Rachel Scott, 17, was an aspiring writer and actress who had recently played the lead in a student-written school play. Sixteen-year-old Kelly Fleming was a quiet girl who liked to write. She wrote songs, poems, and short stories and even was working on her autobiography when she died.

others to safety during the shooting that took his life. His was one of several funerals held that day. "I don't know how we are going to be able to do this," one attendee said. "I can't imagine ever in my life attending two funerals in the same day."[14]

The killers' funerals were small and private. Approximately 15 attended Klebold's funeral. Harris's parents likely had a ceremony for him, but it was not advertised and word never spread to the press.

## Memorial Service before School

The last memorial service held before Columbine students resumed classes was at an amphitheater created amid rock formations outside Denver. During the May 2 ceremony, close friends of those killed in the massacre told stories about those who died. Nick Baumgart, given one minute to talk about his friend Rachel, said: "This has been the

**Mauser and Townsend**

Fifteen-year-old sophomore Daniel Mauser was a straight A student involved in Columbine's debate team, cross-country team, and French club. Daniel had applied for membership to the National Honor Society before his death. He was awarded admission posthumously. Eighteen-year-old senior Lauren Townsend was captain of the Columbine girls' varsity volleyball team and a member of the school's National Honor Society. She had never earned a grade lower than an A. Lauren planned to study biology at Colorado State University after graduation.

one-minute version of Rachel Scott. And, believe me, the 17-year version is a heckuva lot better."[15]

The service offered the school district's administration an opportunity to reassure students before they returned to school after almost two weeks of canceled classes because of the shootings. Jon DeStefano, president of the board of education, promised the 3,000 assembled for the service that the schools would be made safer. At the same time, he said, the school district would not turn the schools into prisons. Furthermore, school principal Frank DeAngelis told the crowd he did not want the shootings to take away from all of Columbine's accomplishments. "I will not allow this tragedy to erase the 27 years of excellence that Columbine represents," DeAngelis said.[16] He contended the school would grow stronger and have a bright future. The future would begin the next day, as Columbine students would return to school for the first day of class since the shootings.

**Principal of Columbine**

After the Columbine shootings, Principal Frank DeAngelis received phone calls of support from other communities that had suffered similar tragedies. Now DeAngelis, still principal of Columbine, makes similar calls, such as one in January 2011 to Omaha, Nebraska, where a student killed an assistant school principal and wounded the principal.

*Vice President Al Gore and his wife, Tipper, attended
a community memorial service for the shooting victims.*

*A nearby high school took in Columbine students during the investigation.*

# BACK TO SCHOOL

After the massacre, Columbine was closed. One reason was that parts of the school were badly damaged during the episode and needed to be repaired. Another was that the school had become a crime scene and contained evidence law enforcers needed. The school year was not quite over when Harris and Klebold attacked on April 20. Graduation was scheduled for May 22, and the last day of school for underclassmen was May 27. The students had to go back to school. But, for the time being, they could not go back to Columbine.

## GETTING READY TO RETURN

The school district's solution to the problem of educating the 1,900 students who were not allowed into Columbine was to send them to neighboring Chatfield Senior High School, which had nearly 2,000 students of its own. Chatfield students would use the school from 7:00 a.m. to 12:10 p.m. each day, and Columbine students would use the building from 12:50 p.m. to 6:00 p.m. Everyone would have shortened classes to make the schedule work. The district decided to start Columbine students at Chatfield on May 3, which allowed the Columbine students time off to attend their schoolmates' funerals.

Among the many problems in getting Columbine's students back to school was that they had left all of their education materials—backpacks, notebooks, textbooks, paper, pens, and pencils—in

Columbine, where they could not retrieve them. Chatfield students solved the problem by seeking donations. In response, retailers donated backpacks, binders, calculators, computers and computer software, and other materials. Each Columbine student received a free book bag filled with school supplies. Chatfield teachers also put together baskets of supplies for Columbine teachers. Before classes started, Columbine sophomore Jennifer Despain said she was ready to go back to school. "I really want to get back and hold a pencil . . . and write a math equation."[1]

## BACK IN CLASS

Columbine students were welcomed at Chatfield on May 3. Yet back to school was not back to normal. "It's really weird," Columbine sophomore Lauren Beachem said. "It's hard going to classes and having certain people missing."[2] Besides the dead, some of the wounded remained in the hospital. They included Sean Graves, Richard Castaldo, Anne Marie Hochhalter, Lance Kirklin, and Patrick Ireland. Patrick was the student television viewers saw escaping the school by dropping out of a library window after he was shot. In addition, the school district offered about a dozen students who were friends of Harris and Klebold the option of finishing the school year at home. Many were concerned about how the killers' friends would be treated by the other students. About a half dozen of these students accepted the offer.

Nonetheless, student attendance that first day was 94 percent. Teacher attendance was 100 percent. Security was heavy and included sheriff's deputies, campus security officers, and parent volunteers. Students were allowed to enter and exit the building only through the main doors. They were not allowed to come and go during the school day. Everyone carried identification cards. Columbine students also carried all of their belongings throughout the school day because they did not have lockers. Counseling was available to those who needed it.

On their first day back, Columbine students attended an hour-long assembly at which Columbine Principal Frank DeAngelis urged them to remember the past but also to move on from it. Freshman student Allison Reardon

**Back in the Game**

Columbine sports resumed before classes did. A week after the slayings, the Columbine girls' soccer team became the first of the school's teams to get back in the game. They won 3-0 and captured the Jefferson County League title. "These kids can survive and continue their lives," Columbine girls' soccer coach Peter Horvath said.[3]

*Frank DeAngelis remains principal at Columbine High School. Since the shootings, he has offered counsel to schools facing similar tragedies.*

said the rally helped buoy spirits. "We were all in it again together as a school."[4] After the assembly, students went to their fifth-period class—the one they were in when Harris and Klebold attacked approximately two weeks before.

## Presidential Visit

Another rally was held May 20 when President Clinton and his wife, Hillary, visited the Columbine community at nearby Dakota Ridge High School.

In his speech, the president encouraged Columbine students to instigate changes in reaction to the shootings. Clinton said,

> *You can give us a culture of values instead of a culture of violence. You can help us to keep guns out of the wrong hands. You can help us to make sure that kids who are in trouble—and there will always be some—are identified early and reached and helped. You've got to help us here.*[5]

## GRADUATION

Two days after the Clintons' visit, Columbine graduated its seniors during a ceremony in an outdoor amphitheater near Denver. Four dead students were missing: Lauren Townsend, Isaiah Shoels, Eric Harris, and Dylan Klebold. A moment of silence was offered for Isaiah, Lauren, and Sanders, the teacher who died. Harris and Klebold were not mentioned.

The crowd of nearly 8,000 gave a standing ovation when the Townsend family accepted Lauren's diploma for her. The family also received valedictorian honors for Lauren, who had never received a grade lower than an A at Columbine. Lauren's mother was also given her daughter's blue and silver graduation gown. The gown had a gold collar reserved for honor graduates. The Shoels, who buried Isaiah in his graduation cap and gown, opted not to attend the graduation ceremony. Also receiving standing ovations that day were graduates Lisa Kreutz, Jeanna Park, and Valeen Schnurr. All three of them were wounded in the library where Lauren and Isaiah died. Lisa used a wheelchair. Jeanna still had bullet fragments in her knee but both she and Valeen were able to walk up to receive their diplomas.

### Ribbon and Tile Controversies

One controversy that stemmed from the Columbine attack involved students who wanted to wear ribbon pins—a unity symbol—on their graduation gowns. Another involved families that wanted tiles they painted with religious symbols to be part of a memorial installation in Columbine. Both controversies wound up in court.

People began wearing ribbon pins after the April 20 rampage, but seniors were not allowed to wear them during the 1999 graduation ceremony. The county had a policy prohibiting adornments to graduation robes. The American Civil Liberties Union challenged the ban, arguing it violated the students' freedom of expression. However, a federal judge backed the prohibition.

Not long after the graduation ceremony, school officials invited people to paint tiles to be installed in Columbine. Religious symbols were banned. Some painted them anyway and sued when their tiles were not included in the installation. A federal judge said the school district could not restrict tile content. However, a federal appeals court in 2002 said the restriction was appropriate. That decision was appealed to the US Supreme Court. In 2003, the court declined to hear the case, upholding the appeals court ruling.

Otherwise, the ceremony was remarkably normal. "Pomp and Circumstance" played. Graduates tossed around a beach ball for a moment before teachers confiscated it. At the end, graduates tossed their blue mortarboards into the air.

## Summer at Columbine

At the end of the school year, some of the survivors of the Columbine massacre and families of some of the victims returned to the school to view the crime scene. On June 1, all of the students were allowed in to collect belongings they had left behind as they ran from the building.

During the summer, the school underwent repairs made necessary by the rampage. Contractors offered to do the repairs in a rush for the beginning of the next school year at no charge. Still, despite $400,000 in donated labor, materials, and equipment, the renovations cost $1.2 million. Renovations included new paint, new tile to replace blood-soaked carpet, new windows and doors, and wheelchair accommodations for three Columbine students paralyzed in the attacks.

Original plans called for the library to be repaired and renovated. But parents of those who died there wanted the library closed because of the bad memories associated with it. So the room was sealed and a bank of lockers was installed in front of it until a solution was reached. A new library was built later.

## Class Begins as Columbine Reopens

On August 16, 1999, hundreds of parents formed a human chain to shield the school's 1,975 students from reporters. The students were ready to begin a new school year at a remodeled Columbine. The day opened with a rally that included the raising of the US flag. The flag had been flying at the school at half-mast since the April 20 shootings. At the rally, student body president Mike Sheehan announced, "We have prevailed. We have overcome."[6]

Parents shielded the students from the media
when the school reopened in fall 1999.

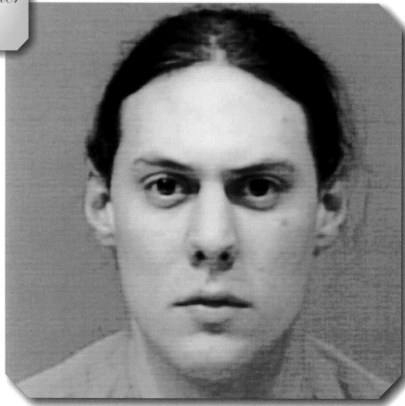

*Mark Manes was charged with illegally selling a handgun to the killers
and sentenced to six years in prison.*

# SOMEONE TO BLAME

*G*etting Columbine's students back in class
and getting the school building repaired
were pressing needs in the months following the
shootings. At the same time, many people—including
the authorities, the public, and those who suffered

in the tragedy—wanted to find out exactly what had happened and hold those who had contributed to the tragedy accountable. Many also wanted to memorialize those who were lost.

Within days of the shooting, authorities knew Klebold and Harris acquired their guns through private sales that required no background checks or record keeping. Within a week they knew Klebold's friend Robyn Anderson had bought the rifle and the two shotguns used in the shootings. Anderson bought the guns at a gun show, where unlicensed vendors can sell guns through what are considered private sales. She then gave the guns to Klebold and Harris. The transaction was legal. The purchase of long guns by an adult for a minor would have been illegal only if the guns came from a federally licensed dealer.

## CRIMINAL CHARGES FILED

However, two others were charged. Within nine days of the shootings, authorities knew Mark Manes sold the TEC-DC9 semiautomatic handgun to the killers with the help of Philip Duran. Duran worked with the shooters at the pizza restaurant. However, this transaction was illegal. On June 17, 1999, Duran was charged with providing a handgun to a minor. Both Manes and Duran pleaded guilty to criminal charges stemming from the gun sale and went to prison. On November 12, Manes was sentenced to six years after pleading guilty on August 8. On June 24, 2000, Duran learned he would be in prison four-and-a-half years.

## The Sheriff's Report

In addition to a minute-by-minute timeline of what happened at Columbine on April 20, 1999, and some conclusions about the episode, the Jefferson County Sheriff's Office report on the attacks includes short biographies on the shooters, an audio link to President Clinton's remarks that day about the shootings, copies of the shooters' schedules for the assault, information about response to the episode from emergency personnel and the media, pictures and descriptions of the temporary memorials established in the wake of the tragedy, and incident management flow charts.

The report was voluminous, with approximately 700 pages of text in addition to photos, drawings, and audio and video clips. It was the result of an investigation that began the day of the massacre and continued until the time of the report's release in May 2000. As part of the investigation, authorities conducted as many as 5,000 interviews and examined as many as 10,000 pieces of evidence.

A judge presiding over lawsuits filed on behalf of slain and injured students ordered the release of the report. Victims' families had claimed the sheriff's office was too slow in releasing information about the shootings to them.

## SHERIFF RELEASES REPORT

Duran and Manes were the only people charged and convicted in the massacre because the two killers were dead. In an official report released May 15, 2000, Jefferson County Sheriff John Stone confirmed Harris and Klebold were the only killers. The report also pointed to other conclusions, among which were:

Of more than 60 people Harris and Klebold listed in their diaries and on a Web site as disliking, only one was injured in the school shooting. And that person apparently was not specifically targeted.

The failure of the cafeteria bombs to explode, which was the main feature of the pair's plan to kill hundreds, led Harris and Klebold to improvise and shoot people instead. No one else besides the killers knew of the killers' plans.

The main focus of the report was a timeline that gave a minute-by-minute account of what happened at Columbine on April 20, 1999. It outlined the attack from the time the shooters arrived on campus at 11:10 a.m. until the coroner officially pronounced 15 people dead approximately six hours later.

## Lawsuits

Just over a month after the shootings, on May 27, the family of slain victim Isaiah Shoels filed a $250 million lawsuit against the Klebold and Harris families. The Shoels alleged that the Klebold

*The family of Dave Sanders laid flowers on his grave.*

and Harris families were negligent because, among other things, their sons were able to build bombs and amass an arsenal in their homes. The Shoels family added gun sellers Manes and Duran to their lawsuit in August 1999.

In April 2000, a year after the massacre, the Shoels family also sued the Jefferson County Sheriff's Office. The Shoels family claimed that if the sheriff's office had properly investigated a complaint about Harris's Web site, where he had written about building bombs and killing people, the massacre could have been prevented. The Shoels family also said the sheriff's deputies who exchanged gunfire with Harris the day of the tragedy should have gone into the school after him rather than establish a perimeter and wait for SWAT members to go in. The sheriff's office contended blame for the tragedy did not rest with it. "Eric Harris and Dylan Klebold were the cause of this tragedy, and the law does not make—and should not make—Colorado's public servants responsible," Jefferson County said in court documents.[1]

More lawsuits from the families of other slain students followed the Shoels's lawsuit. Those additional suits made many of the same contentions the Shoels's lawsuit did. Later, the three people who helped Klebold and Harris get their guns—Manes, Duran, and Anderson—also were sued. Over time, all of the lawsuits were either dismissed or settled out of court before they could go to trial. By the second anniversary of the shootings, the Harris and Klebold families paid $1.6 million into the settlement fund. Duran, Manes, and Anderson paid out an additional $1.3 million. It was the job of a retired federal judge to distribute the money among

the families that settled based on their level of loss.
A year later, Dave Sanders's daughter accepted a
$1.5 million settlement to end her claim against
Jefferson County for allegedly allowing her father
to bleed to death in the hours it took for officers to
reach him. "I hope we can use this agreement as an
opportunity to end these disputes and honor the
victims by remembering their lives as fully as their
deaths," Sheriff John Stone said at the time.[2] It
was not until 2004 that the last of the lawsuits was
settled. Jefferson County paid $117,500 to wounded
student Patrick Ireland to end litigation over
Patrick's claim that deputies stood by
as the boy tried to save himself.

**HOPE Columbine
Memorial Library**

The library built at
Columbine to replace the
one where ten victims
and two shooters died
was named for the com-
mittee that advocated and
raised $3.1 million for it.
The committee's name is
an acronym for Healing
of People Everywhere.
Its Web site continues to
solicit donations for Colorado libraries and victims
of violence.

## MEMORIALS BUILT

As the various lawsuits were filed
and litigated, many efforts were
underway to honor the victims.
On September 10, 1999, a renovated
softball field at Columbine was
dedicated to the memory of Sanders,
who had been the assistant softball
coach. In 2000, as a result of an
effort by a group of family members

The new Columbine library, HOPE Columbine Memorial Library

and friends of the victims, the library where most of the victims were killed was razed and an atrium was built in its place over the cafeteria. A new library, called the HOPE Columbine Memorial Library, was built in another location on campus and opened on June 9, 2001. Various organizations also created scholarships in memory of those lost—scholarships that continue to be awarded in Colorado annually.

A committee formed in 1999 to build a permanent memorial to those killed in the Columbine tragedy. However, because of challenges that included lagging fund-raising, it was not completed and dedicated until September 21, 2007.

It stands in Clement Park, the place where impromptu memorials sprang up in the early days after the attack. The permanent memorial is a stone oval, with an outer wall called the Wall of Healing and an interior circle called the Ring of Remembrance. Inscriptions from the families of each of the victims are included on the inner wall. Some controversy surrounded the inscription composed by Brian Rohrbough, father of victim Daniel, because it was political. It linked the shootings to legalized abortion, an alleged lack of forthrightness by law enforcement officials, and "a godless school system."[3] The memorial committee had asked him to change the words, but he threatened court action. The committee let him write what he wanted.

Columbine survivor Patrick Ireland was among those who spoke at the dedication ceremony. "The world is inherently good," Patrick said. "Columbine shouldn't be a word associated with something bad, with what happened. It should be associated with hope."[4]

### Patrick Ireland

Patrick, known for being the boy who escaped Columbine by dropping out of a window, had to relearn how to walk and talk after he was shot. He went on to graduate as his class's valedictorian in 2000. He later graduated from college with high honors. He went to work as a financial planner and married.

*Columbine survivor Patrick Ireland was asked to carry the Olympic flame
during the 2002 Salt Lake Olympic Torch Relay.*

*Harris, shown here in a video recorded for a school project, is believed to have been a homicidal psychopath.*

# WHY?

In October 1998, Harris contemplated the reaction others would have to the massacre he and Klebold were planning. Harris wrote: "Someone's bound to say, 'What were they thinking?' . . . so this is what I am thinking: 'I have a goal to destroy as much as possible . . . I want to burn the whole world.'"[1] In these writings, Harris did not target black people, Christians, athletes, or bullies in particular. He wanted to kill everybody, indiscriminately.

Investigators who uncovered Harris's explanation among his writings found it lacking. In a letter that accompanied their office's May 15, 2000, report on the Columbine attack, Jefferson County Sheriff John P. Stone and Undersheriff John A. Dunaway said they "cannot answer the most fundamental question—WHY?"[2] The evidence, the officials said, "provides no definitive explanation, and the question continues to haunt us all."[3] Among those haunted were the families of the victims. "It's not going to bring anything or anybody back," said Mike Kirklin, whose son was wounded in the shootings. "But we do need to know. Why did they do this?"[4]

## Harris: Psychopathic?

Many believe the massacre happened because the perpetrators were mentally ill. Some mental health experts said Harris was a homicidal psychopath, or someone capable of killing people without feeling remorse. Experts who studied

Harris's writings and behavior, including lead Columbine investigator Supervisory Special Agent Dwayne Fusilier of the FBI, said Harris exhibited psychopathic characteristics. For example, he felt superior to others and enjoyed deceiving people. Harris also lacked remorse for his bad acts and empathy for his victims. One example of Harris's psychopathic thinking happened after Harris and Klebold were arrested for breaking into a van in 1998. Harris wrote in his personal journal that he thought the owner of the van was stupid for leaving his possessions in the front seat of his van at night in a secluded area. Harris felt entitled to take those possessions in light of the man's perceived stupidity. Another example of Harris's lack of empathy was his ability to taunt his classmates as he was killing them. "Because of their inability to appreciate the feelings of others, some psychopaths are capable of behavior that normal people find not only horrific but baffling," wrote psychologist Robert Hare in his book *Without Conscience*.[5]

Those who believe this theory suggest that while Harris's lack of

**A Natural Born Killer?**

In his journal, Harris talked about his choice to kill, saying it was his fault and not the fault of his parents or siblings, violent media, or music. In the day planner where he listed things to do before the attacks, he also paraphrased Shakespeare: "Good wombs have born bad sons."[6]

empathy allowed him to kill, it was his psychopathic sense of superiority that motivated him to do it. Harris believed most other people were not fit to live. "He was playing God and eliminating unfit people," wrote Peter Langman, a psychologist who studied ten gunmen, including Harris and Klebold, for his book *Why Kids Kill: Inside the Minds of School Shooters.*[7] Harris wanted to destroy humanity but settled for destroying a school.

## KLEBOLD: PSYCHOTIC?

Klebold has been described as a boy who raged and who was depressed and suicidal. In a videotape the gunmen made the morning of the massacre, Klebold said, "I didn't like life very much."[8] According to Langman, Klebold also showed signs of psychosis, a mental disorder characterized by disorganized and unrealistic thoughts. As Fusilier of the FBI came to his conclusion that Harris was a psychopath after reading what Harris wrote, Langman came to his conclusion about Klebold after studying Klebold's writings. In the writings, Klebold fantasized about being a god, spoke of being split from himself, considered suicide, and described feelings of rage and depression. Langman contended

*Klebold, in the school project video recorded with Harris*

Klebold's motivation for killing seemed to be a mix of wanting to die, acting on anger from perceived past mistreatments, living through Harris, and deteriorating mental health.

### ONE THEORY: AN ATTACK TO TERRIFY

Langman discounted theories that Harris and Klebold attacked in revenge against bullies. The handful of bullies Harris complained about had graduated from Columbine a year before the massacre. Klebold did not complain in his journal about bullying. Harris and Klebold wanted to kill everyone at school, including their friends. "It was really a terrorist attack," Langman said, "and they wanted to go down in history for causing the most deaths in U.S. history."[9]

Katherine S. Newman, professor of sociology and public affairs at Princeton University and author of *Rampage: The Social Roots of School Shootings*, agreed with Langman that Columbine was a purposeful attack on an important public institution that aimed to cause terror. However, Newman noted that terrorist attacks are usually symbolic. The attackers usually seek some political gain.

## ANOTHER THEORY: REVOLUTIONARY ACT

Researcher Ralph W. Larkin theorized Harris and Klebold's attack was a severely misguided political move, a revolutionary act that stemmed from what he claimed was harassment they endured from schoolmates. Larkin contended Klebold and Harris wanted to "kick-start a revolution" among students like themselves. "They understood that their pain and humiliation were shared by millions of others and conducted their assault in the name of a larger collectivity," Larkin wrote in an article for *American Behavioral Scientist*. "Klebold and Harris identified the collectivity—outcast students—for which they were exacting revenge."[10]

One Columbine athlete admitted to hassling Harris and Klebold and their friends, whom he referred to as rejects that most students did not want at the school. "Sure we teased them," said Evan Todd, who was wounded in the shooting. "But what do you expect with kids who come to school with weird hairdos and horns on their hats? It's not just jocks; the whole school's disgusted with them."[11] However, Jefferson County spokesman Rick Kaufman contended the theory that the killers retaliated against bullying did not hold up. "Both Harris and Klebold dished out as much ribbing as they received," he said.[12]

## The Killers' Parents

In the aftermath of Columbine, Harris's and Klebold's parents were subjected to blame, at the very least for not knowing their sons were building bombs and stockpiling weapons. But the boys themselves deflected blame from their parents, saying in their videotapes they had tried, and were successful, in keeping their plans hidden from them. "There's nothing you guys could've done to prevent this," Harris said of his parents.[13] Experts said Klebold and Harris came from intact, stable families with parents who cared about them.

Nonetheless, Klebold's mother said in a 2009 essay she wrote for *O: The Oprah Magazine* that she continued to ask herself whether anything she did contributed to her son's rampage. She said she was aware her son did not like school but if he received poor treatment, it did not justify what she termed a disproportionate reaction. The closest she came to offering a reason for his actions was that he was depressed and suicidal, as the mental health experts concluded.

### Profiles of the Parents

Little information about Eric Harris's and Dylan Klebold's parents has been published. Wayne Harris, Eric's father, was retired from the military and worked for a defense contractor. Kathy Harris, who had been a stay-at-home mom, worked part-time for a caterer. Tom Klebold was a geophysicist who consulted for independent oil companies. Susan Klebold was an educator who coordinated a program for vocational students. Together, the Klebolds operated a company that bought, renovated, and then leased out apartments.

Both families kept largely to themselves after the tragedy. The parents were criticized by some who felt the boys' actions had to be the result of how they were parented. Critics contended the parents should have known what their boys were capable of and what they were planning.

She believed he suffered from such severe emotional distress that it impaired his ability to think rationally. In the end, she said, "I will never be able to explain or excuse what he did."[14]

Also in 2009, Wayne and Kathy Harris, Eric's parents, met with Tom and Linda Mauser, parents of Daniel, who Eric killed. The Harrises made no startling revelations about why their son did what he did. During the conversation at a Quaker meeting house, Kathy Harris wept and said several times she was sorry the massacre happened. The Harrises said they now accepted their son was a psychopath but they did not know that about him before the massacre. They were involved in his life but they said they did not know about the arsenal. They were not aware of his Web site rantings either.

Some people expressed sympathy for the parents' plight. In a 2009 newspaper interview, the Klebolds maintained they had no idea their son was capable of such violence. They said he did not do what he did because of the way they reared him. Susan Klebold said, "Dylan did not do this because of the way he was raised. . . . He did it in contradiction to the way he was raised."[15]

The video Harris and Klebold made for an assignment lent credence
to the theory that they wanted revenge against bullies.

*At a memorial service held five days after the shootings, a sign expresses the renewed fear of gun violence in schools.*

# PREVENTING ANOTHER COLUMBINE

*I*n addition to wanting to know why Harris and Klebold did what they did, people also wanted to know how to prevent it from happening again. At first school authorities, acting on flawed theories, focused attention on student loners and students who dressed in black because that is how Klebold and Harris initially were characterized. Experts later said that was the wrong idea because school shooters do not fit a profile. Schools also started antibullying programs in the wake of initial reports Klebold and Harris retaliated against people who bullied them, although experts now say the shooters killed indiscriminately and had no specific targets.

## WHAT STUDENTS CAN DO TO PREVENT SCHOOL VIOLENCE

Students play an important role in preventing violence in schools. They can do a number of things to help tackle the problem, according to suggestions compiled by the sheriff's department in one US county:

❖ Refuse to bring a weapon to school or carry a weapon for someone else. Report those who do bring weapons to school.

❖ Learn how to manage anger effectively by talking out

### School Violence

During the 2005 to 2006 school year, approximately 38 percent of US public schools reported at least one violent episode to police. However, government statistics indicate violence against young people is much more likely outside of school. In 2007 to 2008, for example, of the 1,701 school-age people who were homicide victims, 21 of them were killed at school.

disagreements or walking away from possible fights.

❖ Report crime immediately to school authorities or police.

❖ Welcome new students and introduce them to others.

❖ Mentor a younger student to help that person adjust to school. Be a role model to that student.

❖ Start or join a peer mediation program, become a peer counselor, start an in-school crime watch program, or start a peace pledge campaign.

❖ Report suspicious behavior or statements by other students to a teacher or school counselor.

## LEAKAGE

Authorities are interested in responding to warning signs that someone might be thinking about causing violence. School shooters tend to suggest to others what they plan to do. This hand tipping is called leakage. According to the Centers for Disease Control, in nearly half of the school homicides studied—including but not limited to those who went on rampages—there was some type of warning beforehand. In the case of Columbine, Harris had ranted on the Internet about hating people and wanting to kill them. He also wrote of building bombs. He and Klebold made a video for a class project in which they portrayed their fantasy of shooting bullies. Klebold wrote an essay for school in which students were slain. All of these instances qualify as leakage. Authorities were told about the Web site, and Klebold's essay was brought to the attention of school administrators and his parents, but the issues were dropped later.

In the wake of Columbine, leakage is taken more seriously. Rampage-style shootings peaked from 1997 to 1999, then dropped off. Experts attribute the decrease in shootings to people taking threats seriously and reporting them, according to Debra Viadero in a 2009 article in *Education Week*. Kenneth Trump, president of an Ohio firm that provides school security consulting, said alert students and staff are the best defense against in-school violence.

**Plots Foiled**

School violence plots have often been thwarted by tipsters. One involved a 14-year-old boy who planned to attack a suburban Philadelphia high school in 2007. Someone the boy tried to recruit to join in the attack notified police. In 2008, police were alerted to an 18-year-old South Carolina student's plans to blow up his school by the boy's parents.

He explained,

*The No. 1 way we find out about weapons in schools is not from a piece of equipment but from a kid who comes forward and reports it to an adult that he or she trusts.*[1]

## Prevention Measures

To take advantage of leakage, some schools set up ways for students to anonymously report threats. Many schools instituted other measures aimed at keeping schools safe, including hiring police or security guards and installing security cameras. In surveys of students and school principals post-Columbine, respondents reported the measures that increased the most were security cameras and security guards in schools. The effectiveness of such visible security measures was unclear, according to American University professor Lynn A. Addington. She claimed that these measures were instituted by government officials eager to look like they were taking some action to respond to parents' fears.

Columbine had a surveillance system in place at the time of the attacks that recorded what was happening in the cafeteria. The tapes provided investigators with information after the attack but not in time to stop Harris and Klebold. Columbine also had an armed sheriff's deputy at work at the school at the time of the attacks. He exchanged fire with Harris but did not go into the school after him. Instead, following protocol, the deputy helped establish a perimeter around the school to make sure the shooters did not get out before specially trained and equipped SWAT team members arrived and went in after them.

## PROTOCOL CHANGES

That protocol changed in many places post-Columbine. Where the new protocol, sometimes called rapid deployment, is in place, patrol officers who arrive at a scene to find a shooter who is still shooting must go after the shooter to stop him or her from harming more people. Patrol officers follow this protocol even if it means walking past a wounded person.

Critics of rapid deployment express concern about patrol officers, who do not have the intensive

### Victims' Parents Take On Causes

Many of the parents of the Columbine victims took on causes related to the tragedy. Following the massacre, Daniel Mauser's parents, Tom and Linda, have worked for stricter gun control. Rachel Scott's parents, Darrell and Sandy, founded Rachel's Challenge, a nonprofit organization that aims to inspire "permanent positive culture change in their school, business and community."[2]

training SWAT officers receive, doing what SWAT officers are trained to do. One Illinois SWAT commander said,

> In SWAT, making an entry is always our last option, for when all other methods of resolution have failed . . . but, with rapid deployment, we're telling minimally trained patrol officers to use SWAT's last option as their first option. [3]

## GUN CONTROL

Another response by some to the Columbine shootings was to ask lawmakers to make and strengthen laws controlling the purchase of guns. One such law passed in Colorado as a result of Columbine, closing a loophole there that allowed people to buy guns at gun shows without having to undergo a background

### Columbine: A Rarity

Many efforts have been undertaken to prevent school shootings. However, school shootings remain very rare. Less than 1 percent of the homicides and suicides among children happen at school, according to the Centers for Disease Control. Eighty-nine children between the ages of five and 19 died in school homicides from 1999 to 2005. That's fewer than the 105 children who died during those years in storms and lightning strikes. During the same period, 12 times as many children (approximately 1,100) died as a result of bicycle accidents. The Centers for Disease Control calculated the risk of a child being killed in a school shooting at one in 3.3 million. For being killed in an episode involving multiple fatalities, the risk is less than one in 10 million.

check. Background checks let the dealer know if the buyer has committed a crime that makes it illegal for that person to own a gun. Eighteen-year-old Anderson bought three of the four weapons Harris and Klebold used at a gun show. Anderson was not required to undergo a background check, although she likely would have passed one.

## THE COLUMBINE EFFECT

According to sociologists Glenn W. Muschert and Anthony A. Peguero, school violence was viewed as a local problem before the Columbine shootings and as a national problem afterward. Parents across the country feared for the safety of their children following the shootings. They wanted schools to do more to protect students from violence. This phenomenon came to be known as the Columbine effect, a term coined by *Time* magazine. The term now refers generally to how fear causes the public's feelings about school security and school violence to change after a school shooting. The fear often drives schools to adopt stricter antiviolence policies.

People are still afraid, though school shootings are rare. School shootings are like airplane crashes in that the risk of them happening is low but fear of them is high. People develop a strong fear of these events because when they happen, many people die, Muschert and Peguero explained. This fear of extreme violence can cause schools to focus their prevention efforts on rare forms of violence at the expense of effectively addressing more common forms of school violence, such as bullying. However, students are not as fearful of school shootings as their parents. One 2003 study showed students' fear of violence at school did not change much after Columbine.

## More Than a Decade Later

The tragedy that struck Columbine High School in 1999 made a lasting mark on the psyche of the Columbine community, the United States, and beyond. What happened at Columbine continues to inform how people feel and think about violence in schools and in the media. Parents, school faculty, authorities, and students all over the United States have tried to utilize the lessons learned at Columbine to prevent school violence in the future. It is too late to change what happened at Columbine, but it is not too late to stop this violence from happening again.

*The tragedy at Columbine is an important chapter
in the community's history.*

# TIMELINE

| 1998 | 1998 | 1998 |
|------|------|------|

On January 30, Eric Harris and Dylan Klebold are arrested for breaking into a van and stealing electronics.

In March, the parents of Brooks Brown report Harris to authorities, alleging Harris threatened to kill their son.

Robyn Anderson buys guns at a Denver gun show in November. She gives the guns to Harris and Klebold.

| 1999 | 1999 | 1999 |
|------|------|------|

On April 23, the first in a series of funerals for the deceased victims of Columbine is held.

On April 25, more than 70,000 people attend a public memorial service for the Columbine victims.

On May 2, a memorial service for Columbine students and staff is held.

| 1999 | 1999 | 1999 |
|------|------|------|
| In January, Klebold buys a semiautomatic handgun from Mark Manes. | On April 20, Harris and Klebold kill 13 in a rampage at Columbine High School. Then they kill themselves. | The bodies of ten deceased are removed from Columbine on April 21. |

| 1999 | 1999 | 1999 |
|------|------|------|
| On May 3, Columbine students return to class at Chatfield High School. Mark Manes is arrested for selling Klebold and Harris a handgun. | President Bill Clinton speaks to the Columbine community on May 20. | Columbine's seniors graduate on May 22. Missing are victims Lauren Townsend and Isaiah Shoels, as well as the killers. |

# TIMELINE

| 1999 | 1999 | 1999 |
|------|------|------|
| The family of shooting victim Isaiah Shoels files a $250 million wrongful death lawsuit against Klebold's and Harris's parents on May 27. | On June 1, students are allowed into Columbine for the first time since the shootings so they can recover their belongings. | On June 17, Philip Duran is charged with providing a handgun to a minor. Duran introduced Harris and Klebold to Manes. |

| 1999 | 2000 | 2000 |
|------|------|------|
| Manes is sentenced to six years in prison on November 12. | On May 15, the Jefferson County Sheriff's Office issues a comprehensive report on the Columbine attack. | On June 24, Duran is sentenced to four-and-a-half years in prison. |

## 1999

On August 8, Manes pleads guilty to providing a handgun to Klebold and Harris when they were minors.

## 1999

A new school year begins at a repaired Columbine High School on August 16.

## 1999

The Dave Sanders Memorial Softball Field is dedicated to the deceased coach on September 10.

## 2000

In August, an atrium over the Columbine cafeteria replaces the library where ten Columbine victims were killed.

## 2001

On June 9, the HOPE Columbine Memorial Library opens, replacing the library in which the majority of the Columbine deaths occurred.

## 2007

The Columbine Memorial is dedicated on September 21.

# Essential Facts

## Date of Event

April 20, 1999

## Place of Event

Columbine High School, 6201 South Pierce Street, Littleton, Colorado. The school stands in an unincorporated area of Jefferson County outside Denver and near, but not in, Littleton.

## Key Players

- The shooters: Eric Harris and Dylan Klebold
- The victims who died: Cassie Bernall, Steven Curnow, Corey DePooter, Kelly Fleming, Matthew Kechter, Daniel Mauser, Daniel Rohrbough, William "Dave" Sanders, Rachel Scott, Isaiah Shoels, John Tomlin, Lauren Townsend, and Kyle Velasquez
- Sheriff's Deputy Neil Gardner

## Highlights of Event

- On April 20, 1999, Columbine High School seniors Eric Harris and Dylan Klebold shot and killed 12 of their school mates and one teacher and wounded more than 20 others at school before shooting and killing themselves. Their attack is the worst high school shooting in US history based on the number of people killed and injured.
- The shooters had not intended to commit a shooting rampage, however. The boys' plan was to blow up the school cafeteria at lunchtime, when approximately 500 people would have been there. The plan failed because the time bombs did not detonate.

❖ On May 3, 1999, Columbine students returned to classes at nearby Chatfield High School. The Columbine High School building was badly damaged by the bombs detonated during the massacre as well as gunfire.

❖ Many memorials and candlelight vigils took place all over the country in the weeks and months following the massacre. US president Bill Clinton and First Lady Hilary Rodham Clinton visited Columbine on May 20, 1999 to meet with victims and their families.

❖ On May 22, 1999, the Columbine senior class graduated from high school. Three injured students were able to attend and receive their diplomas. Four would-be graduates died in the massacre, including the two shooters.

❖ Students returned to the repaired Columbine High School building for a new school year on August 16, 1999.

## Quote

"You can give us a culture of values instead of a culture of violence. . . . You can help us to keep guns out of the wrong hands. You can help us to make sure that kids who are in trouble—and there will always be some—are identified early and reached and helped. You've got to help us here."—*US President Bill Clinton, May 20, 1999.*

# GLOSSARY

**amphitheater**
An oval or circular building with rising tiers of seats around an open space.

**carnage**
Massacre; also, the results of a bloody attack or massacre.

**coroner**
A government official whose duty is to investigate the cause of any death not believed to be of natural causes.

**detonate**
To explode with sudden violence.

**diversionary**
Tending to draw attention away from the principal concern.

**empathy**
The action of understanding, being sensitive to, and experiencing vicariously the emotions of another person.

**homicide**
The killing of one person by another.

**mafia**
Any secret society, circle, or clique.

**Nazi**
A member of the National Socialist German Workers' Party, controlling Germany from 1933 to 1945 under Adolf Hitler.

**negligent**
Failing to exercise the care expected of a reasonably wise person in like circumstances.

**paramedic**
A specially trained medical technician licensed to provide a wide range of emergency services before or during transportation to a hospital.

**perimeter**
A protected boundary.

**propane**
A gas found in natural gas and petroleum that is used for fuel.

**protocol**
> The rules of conduct or behavior for a group.

**psychopath**
> A mentally ill or unstable person.

**rampage**
> An episode in which someone attacks others publicly; it involves acts of violence against randomly selected victims.

**swastika**
> An ancient symbol, formerly associated with good luck, adopted as the symbol of Adolf Hitler's Nazi Political Party in the 1930s.

**SWAT**
> A police or military unit specially trained and equipped to handle unusually hazardous situations or missions.

# ADDITIONAL RESOURCES

## SELECTED BIBLIOGRAPHY

"Columbine Archive." *Denver Post*. Denverpost.com, n.d. Web. 23 Aug. 2011.

Cullen, Dave. "Inside Columbine." *Slate*. Slate.com. 16 Apr. 2009. Web. 3 May 2011.

Gibbs, Nancy, and Timothy Roche. "The Columbine Tapes." *Time Magazine*. Time.com. 20 Dec. 1999. Web. 8 June 2011.

Jefferson County Sheriff's Office. *Sheriff's Office Final Report on the Columbine High School Shootings*. CNN.com. 15 May 2000. Web. 13 June 2011.

Langman, Peter. *Why Kids Kill: Inside the Minds of School Shooters*. New York: Palgrave Macmillan, 2009. Print.

Toppo, Greg. "10 years later, the real story behind Columbine." *USA Today*. USA Today.com. 13 Apr. 2009. Web. 10 June 2011.

## FURTHER READINGS

Cullen, Dave. *Columbine*. New York: Twelve, 2009. Print.

Larkin, Ralph. *Comprehending Columbine*. Philadelphia: Temple UP, 2007. Print.

MacKay, Jennifer. *The Columbine School Shootings*. San Diego: Lucent, 2010. Print.

Schier, Helga. *The Causes of School Violence*. Edina, MN: ABDO, 2008. Print.

## WEB LINKS

To learn more about the Columbine shootings, visit ABDO Publishing Company online at **www.abdopublishing.com**. Web sites about the Columbine shootings are featured on our Book Links page. These links are routinely monitored and updated to provide the most current information available.

## Places to Visit

**Clement Park**
7306 W. Bowles Ave. (at Pierce St.), Littleton, CO 80123
http://www.ifoothills.org
303-409-2100
The park includes picnic pavilions, playgrounds, tennis courts, horseshoe pits, a basketball pad, baseball fields, sandpit volleyball courts, batting cages, a lake, and an outdoor amphitheater. It was in Clement Park, adjacent to Columbine High School, where parents, students, emergency personnel, and media representatives gathered during the Columbine massacre and where temporary memorials sprang up afterward.

**Columbine Memorial**
Southeastern edge of Clement Park, 7306 W. Bowles Ave. at Pierce Street, Littleton, CO 80123
http://www.columbinememorial.org
303-973-1209
Opened to the public September 21, 2007, the Columbine Memorial was designed to help visitors remember those who were killed and those who were wounded in the Columbine rampage. Its inner ring is inscribed with the names of the deceased and messages from their families.

**Jefferson County Public Library**
10200 W. 20th Ave., Lakewood, CO 80215
303-235-5275
http://www.jefferson.lib.co.us
The library has many resources related to the Columbine tragedy. Not all of them require a visit to Colorado to use. Some are available for free on the library's Web site.

# SOURCE NOTES

**Chapter 1. Tragedy Strikes a US High School**

1. Julia Martinez. "Massacre at Columbine High: Triage Doctor Horrified." Denver Post. Denverpost.com. 20 April 1999. Web. 16 May 2011.

2. Mike Anton. "Many Students Wounded in Shooting, Explosions, Fire at Jeffco's Columbine High." *Rocky Mountain News*. Rockymountainnews.com, 20 Apr. 1999. Web. 4 May 2011.

3. Ibid.

4. Ibid.

5. Ibid.

6. Bill Hewitt. "Sorrow and Outrage." *People*. Time, 3 May 1999. Web. 12 Oct. 2011.

7. Karen Abbott. "Parents Wait, Cry and Hope." *Rocky Mountain News*. Rockymountainnews.com, 21 April 1999. Web. 11 Aug. 2011.

**Chapter 2. The Boys and the Bombing**

1. Erin Emery, Steve Lipsher, and Ricky Young. "Video, Poems Foreshadowed Day of Disaster." *The Denver Post*. DenverPost.com, 22 Apr. 1999. Web. 20 May 2011.

2. Ibid.

3. Jefferson County Sheriff's Office. "Glimpses of the Suspects." *Sheriff's Office Final Report on the Columbine High School Shootings*. CNN.com, 15 May 2000. Web. 19 May 2011.

4. Ibid.

5. Ibid.

6. Ibid.

7. Ibid.

8. Ibid.

**Chapter 3. April 20, 1999**

1. Jefferson County Sheriff's Office. "Narrative Time Line of Events: 11:10 a.m. to 11:59 a.m." *Sheriff's Office Final Report on the Columbine High School Shootings*. CNN.com, 15 May 2000. Web. 2 May 2011.

2. Brooks Brown. "Columbine Survivor with Words for Virginia Students." *National Public Radio*. NPR.org, 18 Apr. 2007. Web. 3 May 2011.

3. Jefferson County Sheriff's Office. "Narrative Time Line of Events: 11:10 a.m. to 11:59 a.m." *Sheriff's Office Final Report on the Columbine High School Shootings*. CNN.com, 15 May 2000. Web. 2 May 2011.

4. Lisa Ryckman. "Trail of Mayhem: Columbine Plunged into Nightmare of Bullets and Blood." *Rocky Mountain News*. Rockymountainnews.com, 21 Apr. 1999. Web. 4 May 2011.

5. Ibid.

6. Jefferson County Sheriff's Office. "Narrative Time Line of Events: 11:10 a.m. to 11:59 a.m." *Sheriff's Office Final Report on the Columbine High School Shootings.* CNN.com, 15 May 2000. Web. 2 May 2011.

7. Ibid.

8. Ibid.

9. Ibid.

10. Ibid.

11. Elizabeth Day. "Ten Years On and Columbine Still Feels the Pain." *The Observer.* Guardian.co.uk, 12 Apr. 2009. Web. 23 Aug. 2011.

12. Hector Gutierrez. "Smiling, Gentle Giant Buried with Military Honors at Fort Logan." *Rocky Mountain News.* Rockymountainnews.com, 28 Apr. 1999. Web. 12 Aug. 2011.

13. Jefferson County Sheriff's Office. "Findings of Library Events." *Sheriff's Office Final Report on the Columbine High School Shootings.* CNN.com, 15 May 2000. Web. 23 Aug. 2011.

**Chapter 4. Law Enforcement Responds**

1. Dave Cullen. "Inside Columbine." *Slate.* Slate.com, 16 Apr. 2009. Web. 3 May 2011.

2. Jefferson County Sheriff's Office. "Narrative Time Line of Events: 12 Noon to 5 p.m." *Sheriff's Office Final Report on the Columbine High School Shootings.* CNN.com, 15 May 2000. Web. 26 May 2011.

3. Dave Cullen. "Inside Columbine." *Slate.* Slate.com. 16 April 2009. Web. 12 Aug. 2009.

4. Ibid.

5. Lisa Ryckman. "Trail of Mayhem." *Rocky Mountain News.* Rockymountainnews.com, 21 Apr. 1999. Web. 4 May 2011.

6. Patricia Callahan. "A Diary of Devastation." *Denver Post.* Denverpost.com, 22 Apr. 1999. Web. 25 Apr. 2011.

7. Stone C. Brown. "The Colorado Massacre: Guns, Media & Racial Hatred." *Crisis*, May/June 1999. Web. 16 Aug. 2011.

**Chapter 5. Saying Good-Bye**

1. Cindy Brovsky. "Tributes Paid at Park." *Denver Post.* Denverpost.com, 25 Apr. 1999. Web. 28 May 2011.

2. Ibid.

3. Ibid.

4. Tillie Fong. "Crosses for Harris, Klebold Join 13 Others." *Rocky Mountain News.* Rockymountainnews.com. 28 April 1999. Web. 12 August 2011.

5. Ibid.

6. Ibid.

## SOURCE NOTES CONTINUED

7. Lorraine Adams. "Columbine Crosses Can't Bear Weight of Discord." *The Washington Post*. Washingtonpost.com, 3 May 1999. Web. 28 May 2011.

8. Al Gore. "Columbine." *American Rhetoric Online Speech Bank*. Americanrhetoric.com, 25 Apr. 1999. Web. 28 May 2011.

9. Ibid.

10. Mike Anton. "Tens of Thousands 'Honor These Children.'" *Rocky Mountain News*. Rockymountainnews.com, 26 Apr. 1999. Web. 28 May 2011.

11. Carla Crowder. "Your Courage and Commitment to Christ Have Earned You a Special Place in Heaven." *Rocky Mountain News*. Rockymountainnews.com, 27 Apr. 1999. Web. 12 Aug. 2011.

12. James Meadow. "Teens 'Radiant, Forever Young.'" *Rocky Mountain News*. Rockymountainnews.com, 26 Apr. 1999. Web. 12 Aug. 2011.

13. Guy Kelly. "In Memory of Lauren Townsend." *Rocky Mountain News*. Rockymountainnews.com, 27 Apr. 1999. Web. 12 Oct. 2011.

14. Virginia Culver and Sheba R. Wheeler. "Mourners Remember Coach." *Denver Post*. Denverpost.com. 27 Apr. 1999. Web. 28 May 2010.

15. Mark Eddy. "We Are Strong, United." *Denver Post*. Denverpost.com, 3 May 1999. Web. 30 May 2011.

16. Associated Press. "Columbine Service Held as Classes Set to Resume." *Los Angeles Times*. Latimes.com, 3 May 1999. Web. 30 May 2011.

### Chapter 6. Back to School

1. Carlos Illescas. "Students Get Ready to Go Back." *Denver Post*. Denverpost.com, 1 May 1999. Web. 30 May 2011.

2. Ann Schrader. "Back to School Emotional." *Denver Post*. Denverpost.com, 4 May 1999. Web. 30 May 2011.

3. Ralph D. Russo. "Game a Victory for Normality." *Denver Post*. Denverpost.com, 28 Apr. 1999. Web. 30 May 2011.

4. Ann Schrader. "Back to School Emotional." *Denver Post*. Denverpost.com, 4 May 1999. Web. 30 May 2011.

5. Mark Obmascik and Patricia Callahan. "Clintons Meet Columbine." *Denver Post*. Denverpost.com, 21 May 1999. Web. 3 June 2011.

6. David Olinger, Patricia Callahan, and Janet Bingham. "School's Opening Day a Bittersweet Event." *Denver Post*. Denverpost.com, 17 Aug. 1999. Web. Aug. 23 2011.

### Chapter 7. Someone to Blame

1. Howard Pankratz. "Jeffco Fights Lawsuits." *Denver Post*. Denverpost.com, 8 June 2000. Web. 6 June 2011.

2. Karen Abbott and Charley Able. "Daughter of Slain Teacher Agrees to $1.5 Million; Questions Won't Be Answered." *Rocky Mountain News*. Rockymountainnews.com, 21 Aug. 2002. Web. 6 June 2011.

3. "Columbine Memorial Prompted Tears, Smiles." *Denver Post.* Denverpost.com, 22 Sept. 2007. Web. 6 June 2011.

4. Associated Press. "Hundreds Gather to Open Columbine Memorial." *CBS News.* CBSnews.com, 22 Sept. 2007. Web. 6 June 2011.

### Chapter 8. Why?

1. Peter Langman. *Why Kids Kill: Inside the Minds of School Shooters.* New York: Palgrave Macmillan, 2009. Print. 32.

2. Jefferson County Sheriff's Office. "Introduction/Foreword." *Sheriff's Office Final Report on the Columbine High School Shootings.* CNN.com. 15 May 2000. Web. 8 June 2011.

3. Ibid.

4. Nancy Gibbs and Timothy Roche. "The Columbine Tapes." *Time.* Time.com, 20 Dec. 1999. Web. 23 Aug. 2011.

5. Dave Cullen. "The Depressive and the Psychopath." *Slate.* Slate.com. 20 Apr. 2004. Web. 3 May 2011.

6. Jefferson County Sheriff's Office. "Introduction/Foreword." *Sheriff's Office Final Report on the Columbine High School Shootings.* CNN.com, 15 May 2000. Web. 8 June 2011.

7. Peter Langman. *Why Kids Kill: Inside the Minds of School Shooters.* New York: Palgrave Macmillan, 2009. Print. 32.

8. Nancy Gibbs and Timothy Roche. "The Columbine Tapes." *Time.* Time.com, 20 Dec. 1999. Web. 8 June 2011.

9. Debra Viadero. "Lessons Sifted from Tragedy at Columbine." *Education Week* 28.28 (2009): 13. Print.

10. Ralph W. Larkin. "The Columbine Legacy: Rampage Shootings as Political Acts." *American Behavioral Scientist* 52.9 (2009): 1320. Print.

11. Nancy Gibbs and Timothy Roche. "The Columbine Tapes." *Time.* Time.com, 20 Dec. 1999. Web. 23 Aug. 2011.

12. Ibid.

13. Ibid.

14. Susan Klebold. "I Will Never Know Why." *O, The Oprah Magazine.* Oprah.com, Nov. 2009. Web. 9 June 2011.

15. David Brooks. "Columbine: Parents Of a Killer." *New York Times.* New York Times, 15 May 2004. Web. 23 Aug. 2011.

### Chapter 9. Preventing Another Columbine

1. John D. Sutter. "Columbine Massacre Changed School Security." *CNN.* CNN.com, 20 Apr. 2009. Web. 16 May 2011.

2. "Our Mission." *Rachel's Challenge.* Rachelschallenge.org, 2011. Web. 13 Aug. 2011.

3. "Rapid Deployment as a Response to an Active Shooter Incident." *Illinois State Police Academy.* Scribd.com, 2003.Web. 9 June 2011.

# INDEX

# ABOUT THE AUTHOR

Diane Marczely Gimpel is a journalist who formerly covered government, politics, and the courts for *The Intelligencer* newspaper in Doylestown, Pennsylvania, and *The Morning Call* newspaper in Allentown, Pennsylvania. Gimpel now works as a freelance writer for the *Bucks County Herald* of Lahaska, Pennsylvania, and as an author of books for young readers. This is her fifth book.

# PHOTO CREDITS

Kevin Higley/AP Images, cover, 3, 13; David Zalubowski/AP Images, 6; HO/AP Images, 10, 16, 76, 80, 85; Jefferson County Sheriff's Department/Getty Images, 15, 96 (top); Spencer Platt/Getty Images, 19; Jefferson County Sheriff/AP Images, 21; Kevin Moloney/Getty Images, 25; Steve Liss/Time & Life Pictures/Getty Images, 26; Jefferson County Sheriff's Department/AP Images, 30, 66, 98; Hector Mata/AFP/Getty Images, 35; Ed Andrieski/AP Images, 36, 45, 56, 70, 73, 97, 99 (bottom); Jefferson County Sheriff/Getty Images, 39; Shane Morris/Bigstock, 42; Jack Dempsey/AP Images, 46, 60; Michael S. Green/AP Images, 50; Khue Bui/AP Images, 55, 96 (bottom); Eric Gay/AFP/Getty Images, 65, 99 (top); Todd Warshaw/Pool/Getty Images, 75; Eric Gay/AP Images, 86; Bambi L. Dingman/Dreamstime, 95